Spotlight on the
MAYA, AZTEC, and INCA CIVILIZATIONS

Ancient INCA DAILY LIFE

Heather Moore Niver

PowerKiDS
press.

NEW YORK

Jan
985.01
NIV

Published in 2017 by The Rosen Publishing Group, Inc.
29 East 21st Street, New York, NY 10010

Editor: Sarah Machajewski
Book Design: Reann Nye

Photo Credits: Cover Ned M. Seidler/National Geographic/Getty Images; p. 4 https://commons.wikimedia.org/wiki/File:Idiot_Empire.svg; p. 5 Hulton Archive / Handout/Hulton Archive/Getty Images; p. 7 Science & Society Picture Library/SSPL/Getty Images; p. 9 Universal History Archive Collection/Universal Images Group/Getty Images; p. 10 JeremyRichards/Shutterstock.com; p. 11 DEA/G. DAGLI ORTI/De Agostini/Getty Images; pp. 13, 22, 25 Werner Forman/Universal Images Group/ Getty Images; p. 14 terekhov igor/Shutterstock.com; p. 15 Juan Pablo Jaramillo/Shutterstock.com; p.16 MP cz/Shutterstock.com; p. 17 saiko3p/Shutterstock.com; p. 18 DEA / A. DAGLI ORTI/De Agostini/Getty Images; p. 19 Michael Langford/Gallo Images/Getty Images; p. 21 Florilegius/SSPL/Getty Images; p. 23 Brent Stirton/Getty Images News/Getty Images p. 27 MICHAEL LATZ/DDP/Getty Images; p. 29 Dan Breckwoldt/Shutterstock.com.

Library of Congress Cataloging-in-Publication Data

Names: Niver, Heather Moore, author.
Title: Ancient Inca daily life / Heather Moore Niver.
Description: New York : PowerKids Press, [2016] | Series: Spotlight on the
  Maya, Aztec, and Inca civilizations | Includes index.
Identifiers: LCCN 2016006676 | ISBN 9781499419337 (pbk.) | ISBN 9781499419368 (library bound) | ISBN 9781499419344 (6 pack)
Subjects: LCSH: Incas--History--Juvenile literature. | Incas--Social life and
  customs--Juvenile literature.
Classification: LCC F3429 .N58 2016 | DDC 305.898/323--dc23
LC record available at http://lccn.loc.gov/2016006676

CPSIA Compliance Information: Batch #BS16PK: For further information contact Rosen Publishing, New York, New York at 1-800-237-9932.

CONTENTS

INTRODUCING THE INCAS

Around AD 1200, the Incas settled in the mountains of present-day Peru. They built a kingdom in the Sacred Valley with Cuzco as the capital city. Around 1438, the Inca civilization began to grow from a kingdom into a mighty empire that ran thousands of miles along South America's Pacific coast. As strong as the Inca Empire became, however, it only lasted about 100 years.

Daily life in the Inca Empire didn't include a system of writing or even carts with wheels. One of the main tasks in the daily lives of commoners was growing and harvesting the food needed to support their society. Peru's mountains and harsh weather made it difficult to grow crops, but people living in the Andes Mountains adapted to the conditions. Religion was also an important part of the people's daily lives. Their most important god was Inti, god of the sun.

SOUTH AMERICA

INCA EMPIRE

The Inca government sponsored many festivals for its people. In this illustration, the Incas honor the sun during their sun festival, Inti Raymi.

5

INCA GOVERNMENT

Daily life in the Inca Empire was highly organized. The entire society was structured on a **hierarchy** with four levels: the Sapa Inca, royalty, nobility, and commoners. The Sapa Inca, or emperor, was at the top of society. In the Quechua language, his title means "only ruler." Relatives of the Sapa Inca were the society's royalty. They were wealthy and powerful. Sons of the Sapa Inca could become emperor after their father's death.

The noble class was the next level of society. The nobles' responsibilities included ruling over the rest of the Incas. They worked for the government as governors and officials. They had a lot of honors, such as receiving gifts and not having to pay taxes. A class of people called *yanaconas* served the nobility. This was much like slavery.

Most Incas were commoners, which was the lowest level of Inca society. The common people were farmers, herders, **weavers**, craftsmen, and general laborers. Citizens provided food, goods, and labor to the empire. They didn't work for money, since Inca society didn't use a currency. Instead, the government provided for their basic needs.

A Incas, ou Roy du Perou. B Coia ou Reine. ces deux figures ont été dessinées dâpres vn tableau fait par les indiens du Cusco
C indien du Perou D indienne portant la mantilla E leurs maisons —
F moitié du plan de la Bicharra ou fourneau a bruler de l'herbe icho G profil de la Bicharra
H differentes formes de vases trouvés dans les tombeaux des anciens indiens

N. Guerard le fils fecit

The Inca royalty enjoyed more privileges than the common people. The clothing and crafts shown in this image would have been of higher quality than what commoners would have used.

THE SAPA INCA

The Sapa Inca was treated with great respect because the Inca people believed he was the human representative of Inti, the sun god. If someone visited the Sapa Inca, they had to take off their shoes and carry a heavy load on their back. This showed the emperor the visitor respected him.

The Sapa Inca was allowed to have many wives and children. The Sapa Inca's sons had a chance to become the next ruler after their father's death. However, a new emperor had to build his own palace and gain his own riches.

The Sapa Inca provided land to citizens of the empire. Nearly all the people living in the Inca Empire farmed. They paid a portion of what they grew as a kind of tax. Citizens of the empire also built temples, roads, and bridges. Sometimes they performed other duties as well. This was called *mit'a*, which was a yearly labor requirement. Men had to leave their home for a short time to perform their labor.

This is a portrait of the Sapa Inca Huáscar, who ruled from 1527 to 1532.

THE ROYAL LIFE

The Sapa Inca and his family were at the top of society. They lived in a palace in Cuzco, where the central government was located. By the time the empire fell, Cuzco had many royal palaces because each Sapa Inca built his own when he took over.

Cuzco was one of the richest cities in the world while the Inca ruled. It had royal palaces, sacred temples, and buildings that were heavily decorated with gold and silver. Only the most important people, such as the royal family and

This Spanish church was built on top of a former palace in Cuzco in 1571.

This engraving shows an Inca man among the palaces and temples in Cuzco.

nobles, lived in Cuzco. The only commoners allowed to live there were the servants to the nobility.

Children of the upper class were the only Incas who went to school. They were educated by teachers called amautas. Students learned about Inca **culture**, government, and record keeping. Commoners were only educated in tasks such as farming, weaving, stonework, and daily chores. They learned these skills from their parents.

THE NOBLE LIFE

The daily lives of the Inca nobility were comfortable, and they had many riches. They worked in government, helping the Sapa Inca rule. They acted as advisors and helped manage the people. For example, four noblemen called *apos* ruled the four parts of the empire. It was easy to spot a noble in Inca society. Noblemen had their ears pierced around age 14. Men wore very heavy earrings that stretched their earlobes.

Below the noble class was a group of people who weren't Incas at all. They were the leaders of groups of people the Inca conquered. When the Incas conquered them, they took the leaders' sons and sent them to Cuzco to be educated. The sons learned the Inca ways of life, which helped bind the newly conquered people to the Inca. Once the sons learned these ways, they could become curacas, or governors. Curacas ruled the communities throughout the empire.

This figure probably represents an Inca nobleman with long, stretched earlobes.

13

DAILY LIFE FOR THE COMMON PEOPLE

Most Incas were commoners. Farmers and craftsmen were at the bottom of Inca society. They had to farm the land in their communities and produce enough food to survive. They also worked to build the structures, bridges, and roads the Inca Empire is famous for. Women worked at home, cooking, making clothes, and caring for their children.

Inca families lived in communities called ayllus. The ayllus were composed of family groups, or people who had common **ancestors**. People of the Andean region of present-day

RUINS OF HOMES AT MACHU PICCHU

Inca commoners usually lived in simple single-room homes with a roof made of woven grass. The stone house pictured here is a reproduction of a home at Machu Picchu.

South America lived in ayllus for thousands of years before the Inca rose to power. However, the Inca turned ayllus into productive units that provided the resources the Inca Empire needed to survive.

Citizens of the Inca Empire worked very hard—their only days of rest were during religious festivals. The festivals were sponsored by the Inca government. They included food, a beer-like drink called *chicha*, and religious ceremonies. These festivals were meant to make the common people feel loyal to their ruler.

THE INCA DIET

Each ayllu was responsible for growing its own food. Every person was provided for, even if they couldn't work—including the old and the sick.

People living in the Inca Empire raised and ate llamas, alpacas, guinea pigs, and ducks. Llamas and alpacas were very important in other ways, as they provided wool and carried heavy loads. Inca farmers grew many crops, including maize (corn), beans, a root vegetable called cassava, and quinoa, which is a seed.

The Inca built **terraces** to create level areas for growing food. The practice of terrace farming helped people survive in the harsh conditions of the Andes Mountains.

The Andes Mountains are a harsh **environment**, but the Inca learned how to survive there. They built terraces in areas where there were no flat spaces for gardens. They were also masters at storing their food. For example, they would preserve potatoes by setting them out to dry in the cold mountain air. The freeze-dried food lasted a long time. With a lot of food in storage, the Incas were prepared for **droughts** and **famines**.

DAILY RITUALS

Inca life was full of **rituals**. Many of their beliefs centered around nature, and they worshipped the sun and the moon. The Inca sun god, Inti, was the most important of their gods. Days began with a simple ceremony at sunrise. The people lit a fire and placed corn over the flames as an offering to Inti.

Incas had rituals for important events such as the birth of a new child. Both parents performed rituals so their

Incas pray at the Temple of the Sun in Cuzco.

The Incas began each day with a ritual to give thanks to Inti for another day. This object has features of Inti and of Viracocha, the creator god.

baby would be born safely. Later, the baby was named in a ceremony known as *rutichikoy*. The baby's hair was cut and its nails were trimmed during the ceremony.

Other important events had rituals, too. When a boy passed into adulthood, he received a piece of clothing called a loincloth from his mother. Girls had rituals when they were considered women. Both boys and girls were given adult names at these rituals.

MARRIAGE IN INCA SOCIETY

Marriage was an important part of life in Inca society. This was partly because the Inca government only gave land to married couples. Also, marriage was seen as a big transition, or change, in someone's life.

Men and women could decide to marry, or their parents could arrange the marriage. People married young. Women often married when they were between 16 and 20 years old, and men were usually around 25 years old.

Marriage ceremonies were simple. The man, or groom, and his family traveled to the bride's family's house. If the groom's family accepted her, they placed a sandal on her foot. Then, the families went to the groom's house, where they celebrated with gifts and a big feast.

Commoners in Inca society only married one person, but the Sapa Inca and noblemen were allowed to have many wives. To keep the royal bloodlines pure, the Sapa Inca's main wife, or *coya*, had to be his sister. This was not the case for other people in Inca society.

The Sapa Inca, in red, oversees the wedding of a nobleman.

INCA CLOTHING

Inca commoner men usually wore a loincloth and a loose, sleeveless article of clothing that reached their knees. Women wore a similar piece of clothing that was longer and included a belt around their waist. People in the cold mountains wore clothing made of wool. People in warmer environments wore cotton clothing. Even though the climate could be harsh and cold, the Incas wore sandals on their feet.

Some women living in the Inca Empire were very skilled at weaving, which produced the cloth used to make clothing. Llama and alpaca wool was used to make clothing, which is one reason why these animals were so important. Their wool was used to create fine **textiles**. Fancy textiles were one of the most prized treasures among the Inca. They were given to important people as gifts.

The Inca nobility wore clothing that was made from alpaca wool. This piece of clothing is an example of what an Inca noble might have worn.

CRAFTWORK

The Incas created many items that they used in their daily lives, such as bottles and jars. Basic pottery for everyday use, such as eating and drinking, was thick and sturdy. The Inca people also made pottery to use in ceremonies and rituals. Known as huacos, these pieces of pottery had more detail and were made with the best materials. The Incas only used the best pottery for these special events.

The Inca decorated their pottery with bold shapes such as circles and squares. Other pieces showed animals and insects, including llamas, birds, jaguars, and butterflies. Craftsmen used gold, silver, and copper to make important ceremonial objects.

The Inca's fine textiles were an important craft made by the people. The woolen textiles worn by nobles featured bright colors and were decorated with gold and silver thread. The Chosen Women, a group of women who were selected for their beauty, were the best weavers in the empire. They created clothing for the Sapa Inca.

This vessel was probably used in rituals. It's more delicate and has more detail than everyday craftwork.

INCA RELIGION

Religion was an important part of the Inca's daily lives. They worshipped many gods, including gods of the sun, moon, and earth. Viracocha was the god they believed created the world, and they believed his son was Inti. The Incas believed that the Sapa Inca was the human representative of Inti, which is why the Sapa Inca was so important. Inti's wife was the goddess of the moon.

Incas worshipped and held ceremonies in stone temples, and they sometimes **sacrificed** llamas and even children to their gods. Their festivals celebrated events such as crop harvests with dancing, eating, and singing. Priests planned these celebrations and events by studying the sun's movement from their observatories.

The Incas believed in an afterlife. When someone died, the Incas preserved and prepared their body very carefully, creating a mummy. Sometimes they buried their human sacrifices with treasures, such as gold or silver statues or shells.

This mummy was once an Inca woman who lived centuries ago.

MACHU PICCHU MYSTERY

The Incas built some of the world's most amazing structures, some of which still stand today. Skilled stoneworkers planned and built the structures, and men living throughout the empire helped build them as part of their *mit'a* labor service. This included buildings in important settlements such as the capital city of Cuzco and Machu Picchu.

Inca stonemasons built these settlements using only tools of bronze and stone. Hundreds of laborers transported heavy stones from faraway locations. Without wheels and carts, they used braided ropes and ramps made of earth.

Machu Picchu may have been a city built for royalty, perhaps for the Inca emperor Pachacuti Inca Yupanqui, but historians aren't exactly sure what it was built for. It includes plazas, temples, homes, and a cemetery, all connected by walkways. This famous settlement was hidden from most of the world until 1911. It has taught us much about the Inca, but its purpose remains a mystery.

The amazing buildings of Machu Picchu were carefully constructed by stoneworkers.

29

AN END FOR THE INCAS

Fortunately, because of its location, the Spanish never found Machu Picchu when they took over the Inca Empire in the 1530s. A Spanish army led by Francisco Pizarro arrived to find the Incas already at war with one another after the death of the emperor, Huayna Capac. Using their guns, a weapon the Inca had never seen before, the **conquistadors** defeated the Inca fairly quickly. They killed Atahualpa, the last Sapa Inca before Spanish rule, and conquered Cuzco.

Daily life for the Incas changed a great deal after the Spanish arrived. They came down with strange new illnesses brought by the Spanish, such as smallpox. Thousands of Incas died from this sickness alone. The Spanish forced the citizens of the Inca Empire to change their ways of life, including how and what they farmed and what religion they practiced.

The Incas rebelled against the Spanish a few times, but they never succeeded. By 1572, the Inca Empire had fallen completely. However, the Inca's influence survives. Inca ruins still stand throughout South America, and descendants of the Inca still practice traditional ways of life. This **legacy** tells the story of the people's daily lives.

GLOSSARY

ancestor (AN-sehs-tuhr): Someone who comes before others in their family tree.

conquistador (kahn-KEY-stuh-dohr): A Spanish conquerer of Mexico and Peru in the 16th century.

culture (KUHL-chur): The customs and ways of life of a society.

drought (DROWT): A long period of no rain.

environment (ehn-VY-ruhn-munt): The surroundings in which a person, animal, or plant lives.

famine (FAA-mihn): A lack of food.

hierarchy (HI-uhr-aar-kee): A system of organizing social groups in which people are ranked above or below others according to their power or authority.

legacy (LEH-guh-see): Something handed down from the past.

ritual (RIH-chuh-wuhl): A religious ceremony performed through a series of repeated steps.

sacrifice (SAA-krih-fyce): An act of killing a person or animal as an offering to the gods.

terrace (TAIR-uhs): A flat area cut into a slope, often to provide farmland.

textile (TEHK-styl): Cloth, or a fiber used to make cloth.

weaver (WEEV-uhr): A person who makes cloth by crossing strands of thread or yarn over and over.

INDEX

PRIMARY SOURCE LIST

Page 11: Inca palaces and temples in Cuzco. Created by Felipe Guaman Poma de Ayala. Published in *The First New Chronicle and Good Government*. Engraving. 1612–1615. Now kept in The Royal Library, Copenhagen, Denmark.

Page 13: Nobleman figurine. Created by the Inca. Silver, gold, stone, and shell. 1450–1550. Now kept at the Museum of Ethnological Art, Berlin State Museums, Berlin, Germany.

Page 22: Nobleman tunic. Created by a pre-Columbian culture. Camelid fiber and gold. 1430–1533. Now kept at the Dallas Museum of Art, Dallas, Texas.

WEBSITES